W9-AJS-499

Spectacular Animal Towns
The Ant's Nest
A Huge, Underground City

by Miriam Aronin

Consultant: Deborah M. Gordon
Professor of Biology at Stanford University
Author of *Ants at Work: How an Insect Society Is Organized*

BEARPORT
PUBLISHING

New York, New York

Credits

Cover and Title Page, © Pascal Goetgheluck/Ardea; 4, © Barry Turner/Alamy; 5, © Chudoba/Shutterstock; 8T, © Naturfoto Honal/Corbis; 8B, © Mark Moffett/Minden Pictures; 9, © Fir0002/Flagstaffotos; 10, © Paul Zahl/NGS Image Collection; 11, © Mark Moffett/Minden Pictures; 12L, © Dwight Kuhn/Dwight Kuhn Photography; 12R, © Mark Moffett/Minden Pictures; 13T, © Dwight Kuhn/Dwight Kuhn Photography; 13B, © Kletr/Shutterstock; 14, © Dwight Kuhn/Dwight Kuhn Photography; 15, © Donald Specker/Animals Animals Enterprises; 16-17, © Naturfoto Honal/Corbis; 18, © Mark Moffett/Minden Pictures; 19T, © Konrad Wothe/Minden Pictures; 19B, © Gail Shumway/Photographer's Choice/Getty Images; 20, © Mark William Penny/Shutterstock; 21, © Naturfoto Honal/Corbis; 22, © Christine A. Johnson; 23, © Kim Taylor/npl/Minden Pictures; 24, © Mark Moffett/Minden Pictures; 25T, © Christian Ziegler/Minden Pictures; 25B, © Franceso Tomasinelli/PhotoResearchers, Inc.; 26, © C. Rabeling & M. Verhaagh/PNAS; 27, © Pascal Goetgheluck/Ardea; 28L, © Barry Turner/Alamy; 28C, © Rolf Nussbaumer/Nature Picture Library; 28R, Courtesy of Wild Bill/Wikimedia; 29TL, © Martin Horsky/Shutterstock; 29TR, © Joseph Calev/Shutterstock; 29B, © Chris Turner/Shutterstock.

Publisher: Kenn Goin
Editorial Director: Adam Siegel
Creative Director: Spencer Brinker
Design: Dawn Beard Creative
Photo Researcher: James O'Connor

Library of Congress Cataloging-in-Publication Data

Aronin, Miriam.
  The ant's nest : a huge underground city / by Miriam Aronin.
     p. cm. — (Spectacular animal towns)
  Includes bibliographical references and index.
  ISBN-13: 978-1-59716-868-7 (library binding : alk. paper)
  ISBN-10: 1-59716-868-8 (library binding : alk. paper)
  1. Ants—Juvenile literature. 2. Insect societies—Juvenile literature. I. Title.

  QL568.F7A73 2010
  595.79'6—dc22

                              2009003065

For more information, write to Bearport Publishing Company, Inc., 101 Fifth Avenue, Suite 6R, New York, New York 10003. Printed in the United States of America.

10 9 8 7 6 5 4 3 2 1

Contents

A Spectacular Discovery

In 2005, forest workers in Northumberland, England, made a spectacular discovery. Wood ants in a forest there had built an **anthill** out of spruce and pine tree needles that was five and a half feet (1.7 m) tall.

"I couldn't believe its sheer **scale**," said forest worker Steve Morris. Most of the anthills he had seen were no more than two feet (.6 m) tall.

Wood ants

This giant anthill, however, was only the entrance to the wood ants' huge home. Tunnels starting in the anthill led to a hidden underground nest that was home to a **colony** of about 500,000 wood ants!

A large anthill built by wood ants

Wood ants spend time in their aboveground anthill only in the summer. During the cold winter, the ants live in their underground nest, where it is warmer.

Nest Builders

The forest workers in Northumberland called their discovery the ant "Empire State Building." The giant anthill reminded the workers of the famous New York City skyscraper. The nest underneath, however, was more like an entire city.

Ants Around the World

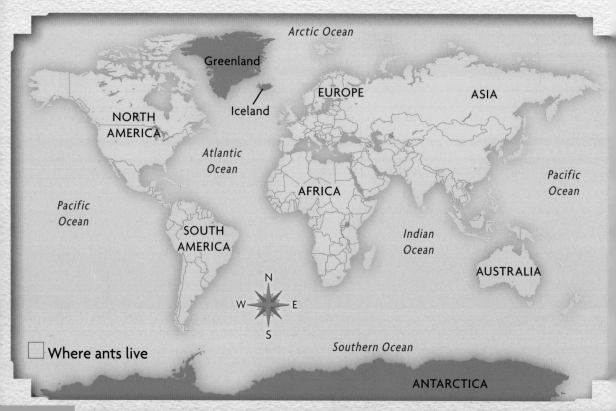

Arctic Ocean

Greenland

Iceland

EUROPE

ASIA

NORTH AMERICA

Atlantic Ocean

Pacific Ocean

AFRICA

Pacific Ocean

SOUTH AMERICA

Indian Ocean

AUSTRALIA

N
W — E
S

☐ Where ants live

Southern Ocean

ANTARCTICA

nd all over t
he coldest a

Just as human cities are made up of many buildings, ant nests are made up of many **chambers**. In each chamber, the **insects** perform a different task to meet the colony's needs.

In some chambers, adult ants care for the colony's young. They feed and wash the young ants to make sure that they grow up healthy. Ants use other chambers to store food. There are even chambers just for resting.

An Ant's Nest

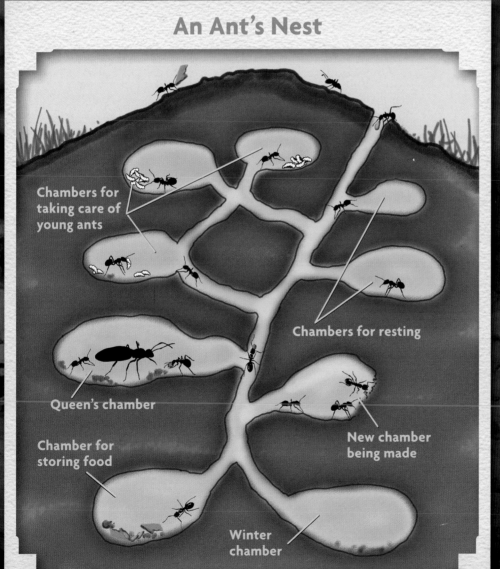

Chambers for taking care of young ants

Chambers for resting

Queen's chamber

Chamber for storing food

New chamber being made

Winter chamber

People build streets and roads to connec buildings in a city. A dig tunnels to conne the chambers in their nest.

Everyone Has a Job

Three kinds of ants live in a colony: workers, males, and the queen. Just as people in a city have different jobs, so do the different kinds of ants in a colony.

ker ants gather
such as seeds
ther insects.

Worker wood
attacking a ca

A worker harvester
ant carrying a seed

Most ants in a colony are workers. They are always females. Worker ants have many different jobs. They build the nest, gather food from outside, and defend their colony from attacks by other ant colonies. They also take care of the colony's young and clean the nest.

Male ants do not do any work in the colony. However, they do have one very important job—to leave the nest and **mate** with queens from other colonies.

In some species, worker ants change jobs as they grow older. Younger workers care for eggs and young ants. Older workers do more dangerous jobs, such as collecting food and protecting the colony.

Ants such as this bull ant can use their powerful jaws to bite attackers, including ants from other colonies.

The Queen of the Colony

Some ant colonies have one queen. Others have several queens. A queen ant spends most of her time in the nest laying eggs. In most colonies, all the workers, young queens, and males in a nest are her **offspring**. Sometimes, however, workers also lay eggs—but these eggs develop only into male ants.

This queen ant scooped up so[me] eggs in her jaw[s in] order to move [them].

Queen ants have their own special chambers for laying eggs. In large colonies, a queen ant can produce thousands of eggs every year.

Without a queen to produce new ants, a colony cannot continue to survive. A colony with only one queen will eventually die off after its queen dies.

Luckily, queen ants live much longer than workers and males. For example, harvester ant workers live for about 1 year, and harvester males may live only a few weeks. Harvester queens, however, can live for 20 years.

A queen ant is usually larger than the other ants in the colony because her body produces eggs.

Growing Up in the Colony

About a week after a queen lays her eggs, they hatch into white worm-like **larvae**. These little creatures have no eyes, legs, or **antennae**. However, they do have tiny mouths for eating. Worker ants feed the helpless larvae to help them grow.

Ant larvae

A worker ant feeding a larva

Workers give some larvae extra food. These larvae grow into queens that will leave the nest to start their own colonies.

After about three weeks, the larvae begin to change into **pupae**. In some ant species, the larvae first spin silk to make coverings for their bodies called cocoons. Other kinds of ants have a tough layer of skin around their bodies when they are pupae.

During the pupal stage, the young insects grow eyes, legs, and antennae. They look like curled-up white ants. After about three weeks, the pupae have finished changing. Fully grown ants come out of their cocoons or skins, ready to join the colony.

Pupae do not eat or move, but they continue to grow.

An adult ant

Starting a New Colony

Most ant eggs grow into workers. Some, however, become males, and a few become queens. Males and young queens of most species have wings. When they are ready to mate, the queens and males fly out of their nests. They will mate with ants from other colonies. If a queen doesn't have wings, she will walk out of the colony to find a male ant from another colony to mate with.

After mating, this queen ant will shed her wings because she no longer needs them. She will spend the rest of her life in her underground nest.

A queen mates only one time during her life. However, she can keep laying up to 1,000 eggs per day for many years.

After a young queen mates, she begins a new colony of her own. She starts by digging a small underground nest. Then she lays her eggs.

The queen cares for her first eggs and larvae until they become adult workers. These workers then take care of the new eggs that the queen lays. Workers also dig more tunnels and chambers to make room for the growing colony.

To make more space in their nest, worker ants dig tunnels and chambers and carry the dirt outside with their jaws.

Ant Communication

Over time, colonies grow to include hundreds, thousands, or even millions of ants. To work together, these ants have to communicate with one another.

The main way ants communicate is through their sense of smell. An ant's antennae help it smell chemicals, called **pheromones**, that an ant's body makes. Ants release pheromones into the air or on the ground.

Ants gather information by touching and smelling things—including one another—with their sensitive antennae.

Some ants use pheromones to share information. When one ant finds food, such as a dead insect, it leaves a pheromone trail on the ground back to its nest. Other ants from the nest can then follow the trail to help collect the food.

Underground Farms

Some kinds of ants do not gather food outside their nests. Instead, they grow it in their underground homes. Leaf-cutter ants grow their main food, **fungus**, inside their huge nests. The nests can be as deep as 18 feet (5.5 m) underground, with up to 3,000 chambers. The damp air inside the nests provides a good environment for growing fungus.

A leaf-cutter ant in its fungus garden

Like human farmers, leaf-cutter ants work hard to tend their "farms." Some worker ants collect leaves and carry them back to the nest in their jaws. They then crush the leaves and place them on the fungus garden. The crushed leaves **fertilize** the soil to help the fungus grow.

Leaf-cutter ants use their sharp jaws to cut leaves. Their jaws act like power saws, moving 1,000 times per second!

Leaf-cutter ants bringing leaves back to their nests

Storing Honeydew

Dairy ants are another kind of ant "farmer." Instead of fungus, however, they "farm" tiny insects called **aphids**.

Dairy ants eat **honeydew**, a sweet liquid produced by aphids. Sometimes the ants collect honeydew that the aphids have left on leaves. Other times the ants rub the bodies of aphids with their antennae to make the tiny insects release the liquid.

When dairy ants use their antennae to make aphids release honeydew, it reminds people of dairy farmers who milk cows.

aphid

Dairy ants got their name because they keep **herds** of aphids the way dairy farmers keep herds of cows.

Aphids are an important source of food for dairy ants. As a result, the ants protect the aphids from **predators**, such as ladybugs. To keep the aphids from flying away, dairy ants bite their wings short. This keeps the ants' food source nearby.

A dairy ant attacking a ladybug

Ant Invasion

Most ants, including leaf-cutters and dairy ants, build their own nests. Some species, however, act as **parasites**. They take over the nests of other ant species and set up their own colonies.

Queens from one North American parasite species move into the nest of another species without hurting any ants there, including the queen. They do, however, lay eggs in the new colony. The workers in the nest care for the eggs.

These gold-colored parasite ant queens have moved in with a larger queen.

The queen of one African parasite species is more violent. When she arrives in another colony, she kills the queen by biting off her head. Then she lays her own eggs. Soon, workers are taking care of the new queen's young.

Some kinds of ants attack other colonies. They bring back "slaves" from those nests to find food and care for the queen and young of their own colony.

This ant is bringing back a "slave" to work in its colony.

An Unstoppable Army

Unlike most ant species, army ants do not build or live in complex nests or anthills. Instead, they create temporary nests as they travel from place to place in their hunt for food. More than 100,000 army ants may march together in a huge line that is 45 feet (13.7 m) wide.

The temporary nests of army ants are made from their own bodies. The ants link their legs and jaws together to form "walls" that protect the colony's queen and her eggs.

An army ant nest

Teamwork allows army ant colonies to attack and kill animals much larger than themselves for food. Ants at the front of the line bite and sting insects, worms, frogs, and other small animals in their path. More army ants follow behind. Soon, the **prey** is covered with ants. The ants work together to tear off pieces of the animal.

An army ant biting a human finger

Army ants have sharp jaws to attack their prey.

jaws

Old Ants, New Discoveries

Ants have existed on Earth for at least 140 million years. However, scientists today are still discovering new species. In 2003, scientist Christian Rabeling found a strange new kind of ant in the rain forest of Brazil. It had a pale body, a long, thin jaw, and no eyes.

The ant's bizarre looks reminded scientists of an alien, so they named it *Martialis heureka* (mar-shee-AL-iss HWARE-ih-kuh). That roughly means "ant from Mars"!

So far, scientists have been able to capture only one *Martialis heureka*.

Scientists think that *Martialis heureka* has existed on Earth longer than any other species of ant alive today.

Scientists believe *Martialis heureka* lives underground and never comes to the surface. Yet many questions remain unanswered about this unusual ant. What does its nest look like? How does it form colonies? What does it eat? Scientists still have a lot to learn about the world's many ant species and their spectacular towns.

There are so many ants on Earth that their total weight is probably greater than the combined weight of all humans.

Ant Colony Facts

Ants are social insects, which means that they live together in colonies. Here are some more facts about ants and their spectacular towns.

	Southern wood ant	Red harvester ant	Texas leaf-cutting ant
Length	.18–.43 inch (4.6–10.9 mm)	.25–.50 inch (6.4–12.7 mm)	.17–.50 inch (4.3–12.7 mm)
Color	reddish	red to dark brown	rust brown to dark brown
Food	insects, honeydew	seeds, dead insects	fungus
Colony Size	more than 250,000	10,000–12,000	3 million– 8 million
Habitat	southern England	western United States	Texas and Louisiana

More Animal Towns

Ants are not the only insects that build and live in nests. Here are two others.

Termites

- Some kinds of termites build nests in trees. Others build underground nests in soil. Still others build nest mounds above the ground that can be up to 20 feet (6 m) tall.
- Termites keep their nests very damp but build openings to allow air to flow in and out.
- There are three kinds of termites in each colony: workers, soldiers, and reproductives that mate and produce young. Each type includes both males and females.
- Inside their dark nests, termites communicate with other members of their colonies through motion, touch, and smell.

termite nest mound

Paper Wasps

- Paper wasps are insects that live in colonies made up of queens, males, and workers (which are all female).
- Queens and workers build nests by chewing wood into a paste, which dries into a paper-like material.
- Paper wasps build nests under roofs or other coverings to protect them from bad weather.
- Nests usually include about 20 to 30 adults, plus 100 to 200 small six-sided hollow spaces for larvae.

Glossary

antennae (an-TEN-ee) the two body parts on an insect's head used for feeling and smelling

anthill (ANT-hil) a mound of earth, pine needles, or other material formed by a colony of ants to serve as the entrance to their nest

aphids (AY-fidz) small insects that eat the juices of plants

chambers (CHAYM-burz) closed-in spaces or rooms, as in part of an insect's nest

colony (KOL-uh-nee) a group of related insects that are all the offspring of the same queen or queens

fertilize (FUR-tuh-*lize*) to add nourishment to soil to help plants grow

fungus (FUHN-guhss) a plant-like organism, such as a mushroom, that does not have roots, flowers, or leaves

herds (HURDZ) large groups of animals

honeydew (HUHN-ee-doo) a sweet substance released by some plant-sucking insects

insects (IN-sekts) small animals that have six legs, three main body parts, two antennae, and a hard covering called an exoskeleton

larvae (LAR-vee) the worm-like form of many kinds of young insects at the stage of development between eggs and pupae

mate (MAYT) to come together to produce offspring

offspring (AWF-spring) an animal's young

parasites (PA-ruh-*sites*) plants or animals that get food by living on or in another plant or animal

pheromones (FAIR-uh-*mohnz*) chemicals with a scent produced by animals to send a message to other animals

predators (PRED-uh-turz) animals that hunt and kill other animals for food

prey (PRAY) an animal that is hunted by another animal for food

pupae (PYOO-pee) young insects in a form between larvae and adults; they are usually enclosed in a cocoon

scale (SKAYL) size, as compared to something else

species (SPEE-sheez) groups that animals are divided into, according to similar characteristics; members of the same species can have offspring together

Bibliography

Chadwick, Alex. "The Savage, Beautiful World of Army Ants." NPR.org (July 25, 2006).

Chang, Kenneth. "Scientists Find One Specimen of Bizarre Primitive Ant." *The New York Times* (September 17, 2008).

Hölldobler, Bert, and Edward O. Wilson. *Journey to the Ants: A Story of Scientific Exploration.* Cambridge, MA: Belknap Press (1998).

Lumpkin, Susan, and Stephanie Hsia. "The First Farmers." *ZooGoer* (July/August 2004).

McClintock, Jack. "The Secret Life of Ants." *Discover Magazine* (November 7, 2003).

Read More

Dyer, Hadley, and Bobbie Kalman. *The Life Cycle of an Ant.* New York: Crabtree Publishing Company (2006).

Lockwood, Sophie. *Ants.* Mankato, MN: Child's World (2008).

Micucci, Charles. *The Life and Times of the Ant.* Boston: Houghton Mifflin Company (2003).

Squire, Ann O. *Ants (A True Book).* New York: Children's Press (2003).

Learn More Online

To learn more about ants and their colonies, visit
www.bearportpublishing.com/SpectacularAnimalTowns

Index

About the Author

Miriam Aronin is a writer and editor. She enjoys reading, knitting, and learning about animals.